# THE FRUGAL CARNIVORE DIET

HOW I EAT A CARNIVORE DIET FOR $4 A DAY

K. SUZANNE

Green Butterfly Press

# ABOUT THE AUTHOR

Kristen Suzanne is an author traveling the world with her family on a multi-year odyssey to experience other cultures and stay fit while she stuffs her face with their food. (For now, meat anyway.)

See Kristen's blog at:

**HappySexyMillionaire.me**

Twitter: @KristensRaw

Instagram: Kristen_Helmstetter

# CONTENTS

## OTHER BOOKS BY K. SUZANNE

**Coffee Self-Talk:** *5 Minutes a Day to Start Living Your Magical Life* (under the name Kristen Helmstetter)

**The Carnivore Diet Handbook**

**Carnivore Diet Intermittent Fasting**

**Sardine Solution**

**Recipes with Sardines**

**Bone Broth Benefits & Easy Bone Broth Recipes**

### K. SUZANNE'S ROMANCE NOVELS

*Under the pen name, Brisa Starr*

**Lockdown Love**

**His Secret**

**Save Me**

**Sweet as Pie**

**Fake It** (September 2020)

# INTRODUCTION

For a free, printable .PDF of the recipes in this book, email me at:

kristen@HappySexyMillionaire.me

**A carnivore diet is a diet in which you don't eat any plants. You only eat meat and animal products.**

So, I don't eat plants. Well, not usually. Most days, I eat an all-carnivore diet, but I'm not dogmatic about it. I feel great on a carnivore diet. My skin is gorgeous (I've struggled with this in the past), PMS is consistently a breeze, maintaining my weight is effortless, and my sleep is peaceful. I'm stronger and my athletic performance improves regularly as I fuel my body with animal foods. As animal foods such as beef, eggs, and sardines are not inflammatory to the body, my injuries heal faster when I cut plants out of my diet.

Best of all, on a carnivore diet, I'm never bloated. I can go from eating a pound of meat to wearing a bikini. Seriously. No poochy belly sticking out. Digestion is better without plants and fiber, and that's no joke. I can't help but favor a carnivore diet when I experience such good results.

I mentioned that I'm not dogmatic about it though. I do my best to stay carnivore and it's really easy 99% of the time. I work in some flex-days however, because we travel a lot. I don't throw carnivore out the window on those days, it just means that a) I plan better, b) I allow for some flexibility for plant foods, and c) it's never as cheap on travel days (unless I'm fasting).

I've been doing this carnivore diet thing, on and off, mostly on... since January 2018. The times I go off the carnivore diet, I notice the difference almost immediately, such as bloating and occasional pimples. This says a lot to me... giving me hints about what is best for my body. I'm still amazed at the difference in my overall everyday experience when I include plants versus when I don't. With a carnivore diet, I'm getting healthy fats and plenty of quality protein. It's giving me a strong body!

If you're brand new to the carnivore diet and you're curious about how in the heck I eat a diet without plants (and why), then read my book, The Carnivore Diet Handbook. That book goes into great depth sharing my journey on the carnivore diet, as well as all of the tips and tricks I've learned along the way. If you're reading this book, you might already be familiar with it though. And now you want to see if you can eat a meat-based diet while saving a ton of money. I'm here to tell you, *it can be done!*

**The Frugal Carnivore Basics**

Sometimes eating meat can get expensive. That's where the frugal carnivore diet comes in. You can save a lot of money eating a carnivore diet if you follow the guidelines in this book. Spoiler alert, and the short version: It's about eating ground beef and no steaks. Day in and day out, mostly.

I usually eat 2 pounds of ground beef daily, which is how I keep my costs to under $4 a day most of the time. (I prefer 80/20 ground beef, meaning 20% fat... no super lean beef if I can avoid it.) Price variations depend on sales and where I happen to be living at the time – as I mentioned above, we travel a lot. I'm fairly active but not overly active by any means. If I were exercising a lot more, I might eat more beef. I'm a 124-lb woman; if I were a low- to moderately-active man, I might eat 2 to 3 pounds on average a day. If I were a highly active man, I might eat 3 to 4 pounds a day. If I were a big and active man (like Dr. Shawn Baker, who is responsible for making the carnivore diet so popular these days) then I might eat 4 to 6 pounds of beef a day. Keep this in mind when calculating costs. Your mileage may vary. But, in general, following these principles will help you make this a frugal diet.

**From Ribeye to Beef Patty**

I love my frugal carnivore diet. I should clarify, I love it now. I used to eat ribeyes every day when I first started this diet. What's not to love about that? Ribeyes are delicious, rich, and full of flavor. If I waited for sales, it's true that I could find them for relatively cheap prices – $6 a pound. That's $12 a day – not super frugal in general terms but frugal in ribeye terms.

This was going great for a while. I was living the ribeye high life. Then my 2-ribeyes-a-day habit all came crashing down when we sold all of our stuff to travel the world - living a digital nomad life.

Steaks are usually more expensive in Europe. They don't have $6 a pound sales like they do in the good ol' U.S. of A. They do, however, have ground beef really cheap (less than $2 a pound), if you shop in the right stores. That was my ticket to eating a frugal carnivore diet for only $4 a day. I mentioned that I love this way of eating "now"... that's because I figured out how to love ground beef, believe it or not, almost as much as ribeye steaks. More on that later.

My promise isn't that everyone reading this book will be able to eat carnivore for $4 a day like I currently can. There are too many variables. But I can promise that, if you follow these guidelines, you'll eat quite frugally for a carnivore.

There are several factors that will affect your costs, namely, how much meat you need and how much it costs you in your location. Are you a huge, gym-going lad who requires 4 pounds of beef a day? If so, you might be looking at $8 a day, but I'll venture to guess this price for a day's worth of food is still drastically lower than what you're used to paying. As noted, the price variations will also depend on where you shop. Location of the store and the store itself will determine how far you can stretch your dollar. If you're buying your beef from Whole Foods Market in NYC then don't expect cheap prices. That said, the very act of buying ground beef, eggs, and sardines compared to everything else you normally buy in that store likely will be cheaper! I cringe at the thought of all that money I burned through on things like goji berries and other useless "superfoods" when I was eating a vegan diet. Those days are over!

One thing is for sure. A frugal carnivore diet that costs $4 to $6 a day is totally possible. Learn what to buy and where to shop. Get your system down and then it's just rinse-and-repeat all the days forward. Easy-peasy. There are a lot of us frugal carnivores out there. We enjoy eating a carnivore diet, staying healthy, and saving truckloads of cash at the same time!

And you're not limited to eating only beef, though, it's my personal preference most days. Read on to discover all the foods I eat on a frugal carnivore diet, as well as how to find these high quality animal foods on the cheap.

Chapter 1

# THE FRUGAL BASICS

## Ingredients

Imagine a movie featuring all frugal carnivore foods as the actors. The lead star is 80/20 ground beef (i.e., 20% fat). Red meat – specifically, beef – is so popular and gets the lead role because it comes loaded with nutrition and most of us carnivores find ourselves craving and desiring it the most. Eating 80/20 ground beef becomes the main food to eat on a frugal carnivore diet (more on beef in Chapter 2).

Next in our movie comes the supporting cast: eggs, sardines, and occasionally chicken. I don't eat these as often, perhaps twice a week. I might pick 3 to 4 of my meals in a week to include or substitute the beef with eggs and sardines. I might opt for chicken one meal a week. My husband, however, eats eggs for breakfast every day and more sardines than I do. He likes the variety.

**Honorable mention:** I should mention offal as an option for a frugal carnivore diet. Things like beef tongue and liver can be excellent frugal options. They are amped with insane, unbelievable nutrition and there's a great argument for including them in the diet because they're so damn good for you and so damn cheap. The trouble is – and frankly, the reason offal is so inexpensive – is that most people can't stand it. I'm in that category, despite my best efforts. I can't stand the taste and texture. (To be fair, beef tongue isn't bad, it's just weird. Liver, though, I've been trying for six years to like it, and I still don't.) However, if you like offal, then consider yourself a lucky badass and make it part of your frugal carnivore diet. And if you have amazing ways to prepare it that I must try, please email me at Kristen@HappySexyMillionaire.me to let me know! I haven't given up on liver yet!

Lastly, you have the extras in our movie. These are the foods that might enhance a meal, but they aren't a substitute for beef, eggs, or sardines. The extras are: butter, whole fat Greek yogurt, cheese, bacon, and deli ham/salami. These items can increase the cost of your meals and they typically aren't as satisfying on the whole. They do, however, add a little party to your routine frugal carnivore plate and enjoying them in small amounts can still be frugal. (My husband would include cheese as a main character. Especially melted cheese.)

So there you have it. My frugal carnivore diet entails eating a carnivore diet, without breaking the bank. It means eating primarily three things: ground beef, canned sardines, and eggs. It means repetition and routine. It means easy. It means cheap.

## Rinse – Repeat.

I never thought I'd ever find myself, a self-proclaimed hardcore foodie, eating the same thing almost every day. Twice a day, in fact. I used to pride myself on being a Gemini who loves change on a regular basis. Yet, here I am embracing regularity, and, frankly, I love it. I feel too good eating this way and I freakin' love the simplicity. Part of my challenge being a foodie was that I was always thinking about food – obsessively, in fact. I was constantly planning what to eat, creating recipes, looking for recipes, making shopping lists, planning all of it. It was damn exhausting. Well, no more. You won't believe the freedom to be had when you're eating the same thing day in and day out. Once you experience that simplicity, it's hard to go back.

## Don't I Get Hungry Between Meals? No Snacks?

Amazingly, since going carnivore, I almost never get hungry during the day. (Before going carnivore, I was constantly hungry.) Meat, especially a pound of beef for a meal, keeps me satisfied for many hours. I usually eat one pound of beef between 9 to 10 in the morning and I'm not hungry again for my second pound of beef until 5 or 6pm. That's right, *eight hours* later! I do enjoy a cup or two of coffee each day.

Recall that I said I "almost" never get hungry during the day. Occasionally I do get hungry between meals, and it usually seems to be based on my activity level... taking a three-hour walk will do it, for instance. In such cases, I'll eat a can of sardines or scramble some eggs or have a slice of cheese with a few slices of salami. But usually it's just beef two times a day. Plus water. Plus coffee.

## Costs

Let's talk about the costs for my frugal carnivore diet. Bottom line: If I eat about 2 pounds of ground beef a day, I can eat for *less than* $4 a day. Add coffee, occasional condiments, or a day where I include a can of sardines, then it ends up being $4. The goal is to find 80/20 ground beef for $2 a pound or less. Everything hinges on that.

Sardines should cost you a $1 a can or less. I often find them for as low as .50 a can, depending on my location in the world, and then I buy as many as I can carry. Sometimes they're more than a buck a can, in which case, you might want to keep looking or buy online (more on this below).

Eggs run from 10 to 20 cents per egg. That means I can eat 5 eggs and a can of sardines for a meal, for two dollars or less.

If you eat a meal of one pound of ground beef, then you're spending $2 or less. Do that twice a day, and you're eating like me. Some women prefer to only eat 3/4 of a pound per meal (twice a day). Some people will want more.

Therefore, between the main frugal carnivore foods of ground beef, eggs, and sardines, you can easily feed yourself for $4 to $6 a day, depending on how much you eat.

### Tip: Intermittent Fasting for Frugality

Some people find it easier to consume only two pounds a day of ground beef if they fast and eat one meal a day. You're still getting a good number of calories and solid nutrition, but by eating a huge meal you stuff yourself and don't even want to eat for another 24 hours. I don't do this often because I can't seem to get myself to eat two pounds in one sitting, or go a whole day without eating in order to get hungry enough to do that. I have read about people doing it regularly though. They call it "intermittent feasting" instead of intermittent fasting. I love the idea though.

I do, however, implement a feasting/fasting sort of protocol on travel days, which is helpful for keeping food costs lower. As I mentioned, we're traveling the world and I'm currently writing this book while living in England. We like to travel by housesitting for people. This is another super cheap living (and travel) secret. (I'll plug my book: *How to Win at House Sitting*, which teaches you how to live rent-free while traveling the world and housesitting.) So, as we housesit our way around the world, we typically move every few weeks. Travel days can be long and eating in restaurants gets expensive fast. So my frugal travel eating tips are as follows: I feast before heading out the door - eating a bit more than I want, so that I don't even want to think about food for 10 hours! And, should I find myself desiring something to munch on, as can happen when traveling and sitting on long train or plane rides, I enjoy a whole-milk cappuccino. It's often enough to take the edge off and bridge the hours and satisfy me between meals.

Back to regular non-travel days... For condiments or items you don't eat often, the prices vary and only add on pennies per meal. From a squirt of mustard to a few slices of jalapeños or a half cup of whole-fat Greek yogurt, you can add more flavor and variety, if you want. Don't forget sea salt - I use plenty of it but that price, again, is barely pennies per serving. Financially, they're rounding error. But they add just enough flavor, pizzazz, and diversity that they can really make a carnivore diet doable for those who would have a hard time being satisfied eating plain meat.

**Frugal Carnivore Tip: MyGroceryDeals.com**

The first thing I do when trying to save money buying food is point my browser to MyGroceryDeals.com. Enter your zip code and look for ground beef. You'll see all the local stores with the cheapest prices at that moment. It's like *magic!...* all the sales are listed there. Also look in your mail for local weekly sales mailers so you can see what prices will be the following week. This can help you plan better.

When I'm traveling in the United Kingdom, I regularly get super cheap prices on ground beef, sardines, and eggs. I find them in stores like Tesco, Morrison's, and Lidl. When I'm in the United States it depends on the store and the location of that store. I'd first start with your local supermarket and see what prices they have for these items. Next I'd look at big grocery stores and superstores like Walmart. There, you can find these frugal carnivore foods and again, pay attention to sales. If the everyday prices aren't cheap, plan your shopping around the sales.

Another great option is to look at membership stores and bulk buying stories like Sam's Club and Costco. These stores are great for finding cheap prices on all of the carnivore staples I've mentioned. These stores do require that you pay an annual membership fee, but it can quickly pay for itself in savings, especially if you buy other items there such as clothes and household items. I remember an episode of Oprah when she was at one of these stores. She called all the items "might as well." Need 800 rolls of toilet paper for only $2? "Might as well." Just kidding, it's not that many rolls or that cheap. But, it's one of those places where the price per item is so cheap that you "might as well" buy in bulk and load up on them!

### Buy an Extra Freezer

Every now and then, you'll see a fantastic sale on meat. You want to stock up, but you don't have the freezer space. If you shell out for a second freezer, then this can save you money in the long run. It costs money upfront to buy the freezer, but you can find some smokin' deals online, or better yet, check Craig's List for used freezers. Craig's List is a super smart option. Once you get a freezer, you will have a higher energy bill so keep that in mind. However, if you have a family eating a lot of meat then it can be a no-brainer to have a second freezer so you can load up on beef you find on sale. It doesn't even have to be a big freezer.

In fact, if you can find a local rancher and buy direct from him/her for 1/8 (or 1/4) of a cow at a time, that freezer will surely pay for itself quickly. This can be a great way to save money on many different cuts of beef because, again, you're buying in bulk. And having different cuts means more variety, if that's important to you.

### Make a Deal With a Butcher

If you're lucky enough to have a local butcher, then you should definitely go in and see what kind of deals you can strike. If you agree to buy a certain amount of beef on a regular basis, they might just give you the best deal possible. Maybe you can talk them into implementing a punch-card loyalty program. At a minimum, a butcher is a great place to get offal and cheap bones for making bone broth (see Chapter 4).

## Cheap Cuts Plus the Instant Pot: A Match Made in Heaven

My last recommendation for eating a frugal carnivore diet is to cook cheap cuts of beef to deliciously "fork tender" in a pressure cooker. Tougher cuts of meat cost less, and pressure cookers make them tender! Get it? Why doesn't everyone do this one simple thing and save a bunch of money?

My favorite pressure cooker is the electric Instant Pot. When you're buying meat in bulk (or you score a bunch of chuck roast on sale), then using a pressure cooker is a delicious way to cook it. You'll get big meals that are delicious and cheap. You can make 4 pounds on Sunday and have your food set for the next couple of days. This saves you even more time and clean up!

## It Bears Repeating: Ground Beef for the Win

I will say that, in spite of all these great tips, I still find my wallet the fattest when I'm eating 80/20 ground beef that I find for $2 a pound. It's easy, I repeat the same meals over and over (which I like), and I don't have to think or plan much. In the next chapter, I'll get into why I never get bored of this meal plan.

## Repetition

How in the world can I eat ground beef for breakfast and ground beef for dinner... and nothing else? Heck, I'm even preparing it the same way, twice a day, every day! Am I bored?

Ummm... no.

Maybe strangely, I'm not bored. On the contrary, I love it.

### My Routine Works

I love it. I look forward to it. I literally smile every time I sit down to eat. While my beef is cooking, I set up a glass of water, sea salt to the side for using once the meat is done cooking, a place mat, napkin and fork. I still chuckle at how I do this every day, twice a day.

I'm as shocked as anyone else really. But you know what? I got tired of always thinking about food. I was tired of planning meals and shopping and looking for recipes. The first thing I noticed a few days into this was how much more time I had and how great that was. The space freed up in my mind literally gave me more energy. I can get in and out of the grocery store so fast. I only need to shop once a week. I never waste any food. Literally, zero waste. It's amazing.

I don't get bored, as most carnivore dieters can attest, because when you're eating a carnivore diet you find yourself only wanting animal foods. You don't crave or desire much of anything else. However, it might take a couple of months to get to this point.

Sure, a Reuben sandwich with fries can sound good sometimes, but I can easily pass on it. That's the important thing. It's not like I'm reduced to eating rabbit food for a diet and I begrudgingly turn my head away. No, on the contrary, I'm eating beef! That's not a hardship. Not to mention, when you notice so many health benefits - instantly - you won't give those up for anything.

The overall health I am enjoying, including the best skin of my life and not ever being bloated, is enough to keep me inspired with my carnivore diet. When steaks are too rich for my wallet, I'm totally game for my beef patties because they taste great and I feel great. Bottom line: What makes it all possible is that I love my food!

When I first came overseas and discovered that steak was really expensive, and that my only option for eating red meat was ground beef, I wasn't thrilled. I had come from the USA where I was luxuriating in fatty ribeye steaks twice a day. I wasn't yet a ground beef mama. But when my hand was forced, I got creative. I found ways to enjoy it. Eating a carnivore diet was important to me and I was determined to find a way to do it without going into debt. I landed on a way to cook my ground beef that I love (see Chapter 2), and it has been my staple recipe since.

Eating a carnivore diet doesn't mean you have to only ever eat meat and nothing else. There are other animal products like whole-fat dairy (cheese, yogurt, kefir, etc). Cheese and bacon can make pretty much anyone happy, unless you're a vegan of course. Bacon isn't always cheap though. Dairy, a little cheese or yogurt... those things can go a long way in mixing things up a bit.

Thankfully, my husband is easygoing and doesn't mind eating the same thing day in and day out. When I met him, no lie, he was drinking whey protein shakes all day long, and eating just one meal of Taco Bell each night (two spicy chicken burritos). Day after day. I didn't know back then how handy this would be in my future.

### Dirty Carnivore

If you're worried you might get bored, another way to stay frugal while allowing a bit of diversity is to be what some are calling a "dirty" carnivore. This is a term coined to describe people who eat mostly carnivore with the occasional plants thrown in. Things like vegetables might be added once in a while. Maybe berries. A piece of chocolate. A glass of wine or a beer. The idea is that the main diet is animal foods. The other stipulation to being a dirty carnivore, of course, is to make sure you don't experience ill effects from eating plants. There are some people who absolutely cannot have any plants whatsoever. But if you don't have horrible reactions to plants, then maybe you can enjoy a dirty carnivore diet and still keep it frugal.

Even if you're generally a strict carnivore, allowing some flexibility is a recipe for success. The carnivore diet isn't a freaking religion... it's just food.

Have a social event coming up? Or does your office do Monday lunch together? You can eat other things and take a more flexible approach to life. I'm not dogmatic about eating this way. In fact, on travel days, I do the best I can but I don't go out of my way or get anxious if I take a day off the carnivore diet and eat whatever. It just depends on you and your situations. Most people, though, find the carnivore diet is too good to stop. Which is really the main point. The very next day after a non-carnivore day, you know what I'm eating? Beef, salt, and coffee. And loving it.

## The REAL Trick to Eating Ground Beef Every Day

So, all this talk about ground beef probably has you thinking this might be a tough way to eat. Fear not. There's a trick to wanting it every day.

The trick is this: You find a way to cook the ground beef that's so delicious you can't wait to eat it. That's it? Yep, that's it. And? I found that way for me. I also found that way for my husband (it's different). I'll share what that very specific way is in the next chapter.

Chapter 2

# BEEF

## Carnivore Dieters Are Beef Eaters

We carnivore eaters are eating a lot of beef. It doesn't always start out this way. In fact, I think many people explore as much animal food diversity as possible when first starting the carnivore diet. This is probably all psychological as it seems like you're restricting yourself, and so you grasp at any and all animal foods you can find. However, one thing in common happens. We tend to find ourselves gravitating toward a beef-heavy diet. Even more specifically, many are eating a lot of ribeye steaks. Well, ribeye steaks are expensive and can add up.

## What About Grass-Fed Beef?

Grass-fed beef is not part of my frugal carnivore diet.

When I initially transitioned from vegan to omnivore, I was militant about eating only grass-fed beef, no matter what it cost. I was under the mistaken belief that grass-fed beef ranchers treated their cows better and that their cows lived happier lives (probably exposed to harp music and weekly massages), while non-grass-fed cows were tortured and miserable. I also thought the meat from grass-fed cows was healthier, too.

I now understand that "grass-fed" is primarily marketing nonsense, as all cows are grass-fed (foraging in a field) for most of their lives, and that most ranchers love their cows and don't torture them. I'm not saying every feed lot is doing everything right, but I've learned that most of them probably are. The main difference when beef is labeled 100% grass-fed is how the cows are "finished" — that is, what they are fed at the end of their lives. Beef that is not "grass-finished" is fed corn prior to slaughter, but was otherwise fed grass its whole life.

As for the health difference between grass-finished and corn-finished, the differences are very minor. A 3.5-ounce serving of grass-finished beef has only 15 milligrams more omega-3 than non-grass-finished beef, which to me, doesn't justify paying the high cost for grass-finished. Instead, simply don't eat chicken or pork and you'll get far fewer omega-6 fatty acids, thereby increasing your omega-3 to omega-6 fatty acid ratio. Or, eat a can of sardines and call it a day. It's important to remember that all beef is extremely nutrient-rich. It has eight times more vitamin B12, six times more zinc, and three times more iron than skinless chicken breast. If you want more nutrition, your money is better spent buying non-grass-finished beef, and eating more of it with the money you save.

## Sidebar: The Trick to Scoring Affordable Ribeyes

If your budget allows for more spending per day in food, then don’t sweat it, just buy ribeyes whenever you feel like it. But if you want to live the frugal carnivore lifestyle, only buy them on sale... sometimes *50-60%* off the regular price! That savings really adds up. As mentioned previously, the best way to find all the sales is using MyGroceryDeals.com. You can often find delicious ribeye steaks for less than $6 a pound (instead of the $10-$14 full price). When I was living in the U.S. and eating ribeyes every day, I always hunted down the best price in town. In an area with multiple grocery stores, they tend to compete fiercely and operate on razor-thin margins, occasionally offering the thing you want on sale, at or below their cost, just to attract people to the store. They usually limit how many you can buy in any visit. But there's no limit on how many times you can visit, or who comes with you to the store! I would visit the store multiple times during its killer sale, or bring my husband (or mom) and have them load up as well. Sometimes I made multiple trips the same day; other times I spread out my visits if the sale was running for many days, as most sales do. Either way, my long-term average price per pound of ribeye was a fraction of what most people pay.

Still, even $6 a pound can be expensive. Most people on a carnivore diet eat 2 to 4 pounds of meat a day. If I eat two pounds of ribeye a day, that's $12 a day for my food. While many people might feel this is a trivial amount, especially when they see how much money they save by not buying a lot of crappy processed food – let alone eating out in restaurants – I'm going to tell you how to make it MUCH cheaper.

## Enter Ground Beef: Twice a Day, Every Day

Ground beef to the rescue. That's right, the humble meat of shitty fast food joints everywhere is now this foodie's personal savior. How did I learn to love the lumpy, grayish-brown blob? Well, I experimented. A LOT. After many attempts, I migrated my attitude about ground beef from bleh, to tolerable, to "pretty good," to "holy shit, this is amazing!"

And now I'm going to cut straight to the answer and tell you how I currently make my frugal-ass, crave-a-licious beef patties every single day.

First, a brief word about 80/20. Don't get anything leaner than 20% fat... this is crucial! Fat is your friend! Not just for flavor and texture, but for nutrition as well. Because you're reading a book about eating carnivore, I probably don't need to tell you that scientists now realize they were wrong for decades about fat. The short version: It's good for you and you need it, so don't avoid it. Health benefits aside, fat makes meat taste much better. Using only 80/20 is essential for making ground beef delicious enough to eat every day. So here we go...

**Recipe: 1 Pound of Ground Beef - Skillet Patty Style**

- I start with one pound of 80/20 ground beef.
- I make two patties if I have a small skillet. If it's a big skillet, I make one big-ass patty of ground beef. I don't over-work the beef.
- I don't need any oil in the skillet, because the beef has plenty of fat. My patties are pressed pretty thin (~1/2 inch) to decrease cooking time, and also to give me a better ratio of external seared beef to internal non-seared beef.
- I don't salt the meat before cooking.
- I get the skillet hot(!), and then I put the patty inside the skillet.
- I let it get a good sear on the first side (about 60 seconds), then I flip it, keeping the heat hot. After 30 to 60 seconds of it cooking on the second side, I drain off the fat onto my plate, where I will eat it with the patty. That's right, keep and eat the fat!
- I keep cooking it until it reaches my desired temperature (137-142 degrees F for ground beef). During this time, I flip it a few more times and drain it, again, keeping that oil and fat that drains off. It's delicious.
- Finally, I salt the beef with sea salt, and I eat it. I do this for breakfast somewhere between 9am to 10am. I do it again around 5pm to 6pm for dinner. Voila, I'm a satisfied frugal carnivore.

That's the way I love it. I crave that delicious seared edge around the outside of my ground beef patty. That was the trick to my loving these patties. They had to have a rich and savory explosive-tasting sear on my patties.

My husband's preference, however is with cheese. (I bake his beef in a baking dish with the cheese on top.) He LOVES(!) cheese and is more than happy to eat ground beef every day, all day, if there's melted cheese on it. He'll add a dab of mustard or hot sauce and call it a "carnivore cheeseburger." (Well, mostly carnivore, since condiments aren't, but that's nitpicking.) And it's still a frugal carnivore meal. His cheese adds a tiny bit more cost than my plain patties, but not a lot.

There are many ways to cook ground beef, and using a skillet is my preferred method. You can also bake it, sauté it into a crumble, use an air fryer, grill it, or cook it under the broiler. Broiling and grilling are great methods for cooking a lot all at once.

Favorite Variations:

- Sometimes I put sliced jalapeños (from a jar) on my patty and a spoonful of full-fat Greek yogurt. OMFG – so good.
- Condiments? Sure. Remember, if you're body tolerates it, there's no need to be dogmatic about sticking to 100% carnivore. My days of being dogmatic are over. Learned my lesson from being a dogmatic vegan. <sigh>

Sometimes I use condiments for fun. They can do a great job at dressing up ground beef. In fact, while I was fine-tuning my patty-making skills, making it my perfect food, I loved dipping my not-as-great versions in mustard. If adding mustard helped me eat frugal ground beef regularly, then I was all for it.

Still don't want ground beef every day? No problem. For those of you who want more variety in your cuts of meat and still want to save gobs of cash, consider buying a nice big-ass chuck roast. Read on!

## Big Ass Roast

Chuck roast can be some of the most succulent and delicious beef ever. There are two tricks. First, you need to cook the beef so that it's "fork tender." Or as the saying goes, the meat should "tremble as the fork approaches." The second, optional, thing is to cook the beef in bone broth. You can cook it in water and that is fine. But, if you want *flavor on steroids*, then cook it in bone broth. It won't cost you one cent more for extravagant flavor if you make your own bone broth, which I've been advising the readers of my blog to do for years.

I'm talking about chicken bone broth here. It's easy to make (see Chapter 4). If you roast a chicken (or drumsticks, or thighs), then you'll have bones leftover. You can make broth from these bones. Now, if you don't happen to have homemade broth on hand in your refrigerator or freezer, then I'm not suggesting you buy it - I'd just use water.

If you find a great sale on chuck roast, then load up. Get a nice big one (4 to 5 pounds) - preferably bone-in for the most flavor. Even better, when you find a super sale, buy a couple of roasts and freeze them.

## Beef Stew Pressure Cooker (Instant Pot)

The time it takes to cook your roast will depend on a few things. The number of pounds of meat you're cooking will change the time. The time also depends on whether you keep it whole, versus halved, quartered, or cubed. Lastly, the temperature of the meat going into the pressure cooker will impact its cooking time. Therefore, the times given below are estimates.

Prior to cooking, I like to let my beef sit on the counter for about an hour, getting closer to room temperature. I usually cook four pounds at a time. I also like to quarter my beef or cut it into large 2-inch cubes. Therefore, I usually cook it for about 60 minutes and let the pressure cooker slow release the pressure once it's done. On occasion, if it isn't as tender as I want it to be, then I'll cook it another 5 to 15 minutes (no slow release this second time) until I'm happy with it.

- 1 to 5 pounds chuck roast
- 1 cup water or bone broth
- salt

1. Take your beef and season it generously with salt.
2. Pour the water or bone broth into the Instant Pot.
3. Place the beef inside.
4. Secure the lid.
5. Set the Instant Pot to HIGH pressure for 60 minutes (typically good for 2 to 4 pounds, not in one whole piece).
6. Let the pressure slow release naturally.
7. Test for tenderness. If it's not shredding beautifully, then put the lid back on and cook another 5 to 10 minutes. Let it quick release this second time and test it again.

### Slow Roasted Chuck Roast (Dutch oven)

This recipe is for cooking a chuck roast in a Dutch oven (or similar pot with a lid). You cook it in the oven at a low temperature for many hours. The timing will depend on the size of the beef and whether you cut it or not. Be patient – the tender results are worth the wait! You might have to check the beef a few times, testing for tenderness and then letting it cook another 20 minutes each time you put it back in the oven, if it's not quite done.

- 3 to 5 pounds chuck roast
- 2 cups bone broth or water
- salt

1. Before cooking, let the meat sit out on the counter for about an hour, so it's close to room temperature.

2. Preheat the oven to 200 degrees F.
3. Cut the meat in half or thirds. Season it generously with salt.
4. Put the meat and liquid into the Dutch oven and put the lid on top.
5. Cook for two hours.
6. Turn the heat up to 250 degrees and cook another 4 to 6 hours. If you need to add more liquid, then do so during the cooking process.

## Chapter 3

# EGGS

### Nutrition

Eggs are a wonderful source of protein for frugal carnivores. I often find eggs for twenty cents a piece, sometimes less. Cook five of them and you've only spent a buck. I also like to order eggs when we eat at restaurants, if possible, because they tend to be one of the more frugal options on the menu. (Frugal Tip: Ordering 1-3 eggs on top of a beef patty at a restaurant usually costs less than ordering two patties, because they're likely to ring that up as two full-priced hamburgers.)

When eating out and eggs aren't quite enough, I've been known to supplement them by throwing in a tin of sardines, which I always carry in my purse, for emergencies. (See my book, Sardine Solution, for more about these little miracle fish.) When we stayed in The Black Hole Bed and Breakfast in Winchester, England, they served traditional English breakfast (sausage, bacon, eggs, mushrooms, and tomato). As I wanted to keep to my carnivore diet as much as possible, I asked them to hold the mushrooms and tomatoes, give me the meat and eggs, and then I whipped open a can of sardines, just for good measure. It's the little hacks like these that make eating a carnivore diet easier while traveling, and helping you keep it frugal, too.

While I wouldn't survive solely on eggs (they don't keep me full all day long like beef does), I do enjoy them from time to time. They add a nice healthy diversity to a beef-based diet. Not only are they a good source of protein, the yolks are super nutritious.

Unlike grass-fed beef, which, as I mentioned previously, is mostly just marketing, free-range chickens are legitimately more nutritious and ethical than caged chickens, so I do opt for them when possible. Fortunately, in many parts of the world outside the U.S., chickens are free-range by default, so you don't pay extra for their super healthy eggs.

In terms of nutrition, my favorite thing about eggs is the retinol. It's a valuable nutrient, especially for glowing skin. Now, if you're eating a carnivore diet and you don't eat eggs, that doesn't mean you won't have great skin. I think a lot of skin problems for people come from the inflammatory foods (plants especially, possibly dairy) that they're eating. In these situations, I think eggs are extra valuable, along with the elimination of problematic foods. This was a key to helping my skin recover when I stopped eating a vegan diet 6 years ago. Retinol is also great for the immune system. Again though, by simply not eating carbohydrates, you're setting your immune system up to win, and the retinol in eggs (or liver) is simply an added bonus.

One of the best things about eggs is how easy and fast they are to prepare. Get a skillet hot, add butter, crack in eggs. Salt. Done. I can make my daughter's eggy breakfast or my husband's favorite egg-n-sardine combo (see below) in less than a minute.

There are tons of ways to enjoy eggs and I'll share a couple of my favorite recipes below. I usually prepare them in one of four ways: scrambled in butter, fried in butter, poached in water, or hard-cooked (using the pressure cooker). Sometimes, though rarely, I'll get fancy and bake them with cream.

My husband prefers eggs on a daily basis for his frugal carnivore approach. His ideal carnivore diet includes 4 scrambled (or fried) eggs in the morning with some melted cheese in them and topped with a can of sardines and a dash of hot sauce. He enjoys a cup of coffee, too. Then he goes all day without food (more so because he's busy and doesn't think to eat). At dinner, he likes a pound of ground beef, topped with melted cheese, maybe a handful of berries or some bell pepper, and usually a beer. He's pretty much a "dirty carnivore." He has gone stretches as a "clean" carnivore, but he really likes his craft beers. So long as he feels great and stays in shape then he's happy. We have both found that staying in shape is quite easy eating carnivore, with only moderate body-weight exercise and walking. ("Moderate" for us these days because our travels have meant no gym access for the past six months).

If I'm eating eggs, then I'll scramble or fry 4 to 5 of them, and enjoy them doused with butter. Good protein and fat! Sometimes I eat three eggs and then top them with a can of sardines and some hot sauce, too. As mentioned earlier, eggs don't keep me satisfied all day like beef does, so when I eat eggs for breakfast, I'll usually end up eating lunch. That's a possible cost to look out for when you're considering the low cost of eggs.

## Recipes

I'm going to assume we all know how to scramble and fry eggs. But, I'm not sure everyone knows how to poach or hard-boil/cook them. I will teach you here.

### Traditional Hard-Boiled Eggs

Hard-boiled eggs are great to have in the refrigerator at all times. They make for the quickest breakfast or mid-night snack ever (even faster than my dear sardines). My favorite way to make hard-boiled eggs is in the Instant Pot because it virtually guarantees easy-peel shells, and it's a hands-off process for cooking. It works every time. (See Pressure Cooker Hard-Cooked Eggs, below.) If you don't have a pressure cooker, fear not, just use the following traditional method for hard-boiling your eggs.

1. Get a pan and put cold water in it.
2. Add the eggs (in their shells).
3. Bring the water to a boil. Turn the heat off. Take the pot off the burner.
4. Cover the pot and let them sit in the hot water for 8 to 9 minutes (you can experiment and see if you like the yolk's hardness at 7, 8, or 9 minutes - it depends on your preference). While the eggs are cooking, prepare an ice bath (a bowl filled with half ice and half water).
5. Using tongs, immediately transfer the eggs into the ice bath to stop their residual cooking.

**Pressure Cooker Hard-Cooked Eggs**

I make these in the Instant Pot, one of my favorite kitchen appliances of all time. The shells peel off so easily, it's actually enjoyable.

1. Put one cup of water into the Instant Pot plus the trivet (rack insert).
2. Add the eggs (in shell), straight from the fridge.
3. Cook on LOW pressure for 3-5 minutes depending on desired doneness (for me, that's 4 minutes). While they're cooking, prepare an ice bath (bowl with half water and half ice).
4. Once the Instant Pot is done cooking, Quick Release the pressure and immediately transfer the eggs to the ice bath using tongs.

5. After letting the eggs cool for a few minutes, you can easily peel off the shells.

## Poached Eggs

Poached eggs are delicious served on top of a ground beef patty or sardines.

1. Get a pan and fill it with enough water that if you put an egg on the bottom of the pot (in the shell), laying on its side, the water would just cover the top of the egg... so as deep as the width of an egg. (If you used an egg in this way to figure out how much water to put in the pan, remove the egg now.)
2. Turn the stove on and bring the water to a low simmer.
3. Crack the egg(s) gently into the simmering water and briefly turn up the heat to compensate for the cold egg(s) and then turn it back down. Cook for 3 minutes.
4. Use a slotted spoon to remove the eggs and serve.

## Cheesy Ham Omelet

This is one of my daughter's favorite breakfasts (and lunches!)

- 3 eggs
- 1 slice ham
- 1 slice cheese
- Salt
- Butter or ghee

1. Gently whisk the eggs. Add salt.
2. Get a 6-inch skillet hot(!) (if using 4 eggs, use an 8" pan). Add butter or ghee.
3. Add the eggs and let them cook a bit. Add the ham and cheese on top.
4. When the eggs look like the bottom part is cooked and you

can fold the egg into a taco or burrito shape around the ham and cheese, then take a rubber spatula, scrape down the sides, and fold it in half (or thirds).

5. Continue cooking until eggs are cooked through.

## Deviled Eggs

This recipe calls for a little bit of mustard and vinegar, but I promise the carnivore police will not kick in your door if you make it. Feel free to omit them though if they bother you. The amazing thing about these deviled eggs is how delicious they are with Greek yogurt instead of mayonnaise.

- 6 eggs (hard-boiled and peeled)
- 3 tablespoons whole-fat Greek yogurt
- 1 to 2 squirts yellow mustard
- Splash vinegar
- salt, to taste

1. Split the eggs in half (lengthwise).
2. Gently scoop the yolks into a small mixing bowl. Set the egg whites on a plate and set aside.
3. Mash the yolks with a fork.
4. To the yolks, add the rest of the ingredients. Mash it together.
5. Use a small spoon and scoop the filling gently into each egg white.

Variation: My mom's favorite way to make these is using any leftover cooked meat in the refrigerator (like cold sausage) and mashing it in with the yolks before filling the whites. My husband loves them with a splash of hot sauce!

## Baked Eggs with Cream

- 1/2 tablespoon butter, softened
- 2 tablespoons heavy whipping cream
- 2 eggs
- salt, to taste

1. Heat the oven to 425° F.
2. Coat a 4-ounce ramekin with butter.
3. Put the cream in the ramekin.
4. Crack the eggs into the ramekin.
5. Bake until the whites are set, about 10 to 12 minutes.

Chapter 4

# CHICKEN

## Thighs & Drumsticks

Chicken makes a delicious alternative to ground beef. I'm particularly fond of bone-in, skin-on chicken thighs and drumsticks. It's my daughter's favorite, too. They are the more nutritious part of the bird, and they're the cheapest. I can often find a pound of either for about $1.50. I'll buy two or three packages and cook them all at once. My family of three (husband, 8 year old daughter, and myself) will feast on them for a lunch or dinner.

I find eating chicken like this satisfying, with all the protein I'm getting plus the crispy golden skin. That said, chicken only has a supporting role in my diet, as I prefer to eat mostly beef. But, damn, roasted chicken drumsticks are so good sometimes! Even better – you can whip up a little batch of bone broth using the leftover bones. More about that in a bit.

## Easy-Roasted Chicken Thighs (or Chicken Drumsticks)

- 1 to 3 pounds chicken thighs (bone-in, skin-on) or drumsticks
- salt

1. Preheat the oven to 375 degree F.
2. Place the thighs or drumsticks on a baking dish or a pan with a lip (to catch the juices). Make sure there's a bit of space between them to increase airflow and help them get crispy skin.
3. Sprinkle salt on top of them all.
4. Cook for about 30 minutes or until the internal temperature, close to the bone, reaches 175 degrees F.

## Chicken Bone Broth

There's a version of bone broth I make that cooks for many hours to extract maximum nutrition from the bones. But I also have a simpler, quick-n-dirty method for using the few bones from my family eating roasted chicken thighs or drumsticks. I just toss the bones into a pot with some water and cook them for a few hours. It turns out great. If I'd like to make a bigger batch than the handful of bones permits, sometimes I freeze the bones until I have a bigger collection.

Using chicken bones to make chicken bone broth stretches the chicken further. It's a delicious drink and I can also use it to cook a chuck roast, or to make egg soup (see recipe, below). Or, sometimes I just sip the broth by itself in place of coffee. (For lots more about this, see my Bone Broth book.)

**Quick-n-Dirty Bone Broth:**

1. Take the bones from your roasted chicken and put them in a small soup pot.
2. Add enough cold water to cover the bones.

3. Turn the stove on high and bring the water to just barely a boil, and then immediately turn the heat down so the water is simmering.
4. Simmer for 2 to 4 hours. Keep an eye on the pot because the water will evaporate as it cooks. Add some water as needed.
5. When you're done cooking, use tongs to remove the bones and set them aside in a bowl to cool before discarding.
6. Let the broth cool a bit and then strain it into another pot.
7. If possible, use an ice bath to cool the broth quickly. To do this, take a big bowl and fill it with half ice and half water. Then, take the pot with the broth in it and set it inside the ice bath.
8. Once the broth is cool enough for storing, transfer the broth into glass jars (or containers) with lids before putting in the refrigerator.
9. After the broth has chilled the fat will rise to the top. You can keep it with the broth or take some off and use for cooking eggs. Chicken bone broth will stay fresh for up to 5 days in the refrigerator.

**Bone Broth Egg Drop Soup**

- 2 cups bone broth
- 2 eggs, lightly whisked
- salt, to taste

1. Heat the broth on the stove to a simmer.
2. Slowly pour the eggs into the broth and stir to create a cooked ribbon of eggs.
3. Once the eggs are cooked to your liking, pour the soup into a large mug or a bowl.
4. Taste and season with salt.

Chapter 5

# SARDINES

## Learn to Love Sardines

Sardines... oh sardines.

Don't skip this chapter. I know you might be thinking gross, sardines? Trust me, yes, sardines. I learned to love them, and you can, too. I wrote a book, *Sardine Solution*, detailing how and why people can and should love them. I wasn't a fan of sardines when I first tried them, but with some time and recipes that eased me into them slowly, I learned to truly love them. You can, too, if you don't already.

Sardines make a great part of a frugal carnivore diet, especially when you find them at ultra-cheap prices. In the U.K. I can get them for 50 cents a can! That's amazing. If I eat two cans, it's a great little meal for only a buck! I can't always find them that cheap in the U.S., but sometimes I can. Still, on average you should be able to score some for around a buck per can. It makes a cheap and super quick meal.

## Tips for Getting Good Deals on Sardines

- Buy in bulk at your local grocery store. At some stores, if you buy a case of something, you get 10% off, or more. Be sure to ask. In fact, ask the store manager if he or she can give you an extra big discount for buying a few cases. Sardines have a 5+ year shelf-life, so there's no reason not to buy in bulk and save a ton.
- Wait until they're on sale and then load up! Seriously buy a lot. Again, the long shelf-life.
- Buy on Amazon using their subscribe and save feature.
- Shop at bulk buying membership stores like Costco or Sam's Club.

Sardines are great because they're super convenient. You can literally eat them right out of the can. They don't need cooking or prepping, if you don't mind eating them plain. You can also find them packed in different sauces. I'm mindful of the ingredients in the sauces (I avoid vegetable oils), but sometimes I find them packed in things like tomato sauce, mustard sauce, or chili sauce. It's a small amount of sauce and you can leave most of it in the can if you want. That said, I most often buy sardines plain (in brine only).

You can travel with sardines, toss them in your backpack, purse, suitcase, or gym bag. Sure, you could travel with beefy jerky instead, but it's usually not frugal and it's hard to eat a meal's worth of jerky. Sardines, on the other hand, are frugal and more filling.

Sardines are also extremely nutritious. It's like a little shot of vitamins. You get a boost of omega 3 fatty acids, B-vitamins, calcium (if you buy the ones with bones and eat them, and you should - even my kid does!), vitamin D, and more.

I probably eat a can or two of sardines a couple times a week. More if it's a travel day because it's the most frugal food I can eat on those days. When we travel in France, where meat is particularly expensive, I tend to live more off of sardines, eggs, cheese, and butter for most of my diet - the rest as plants to save money.

Sardines are also great if you're in a hurry and you don't have time to cook up a ground beef patty. You can eat a can (or 2) of sardines as you're heading out the door. They're fantastic!

For those who don't already like sardines, the trick to getting to the point where you can easily eat them plain from the can is detailed in my book, Sardine Solution, but I'll give you the Cliff Notes version here.

First, you need to stop being a baby and see yourself as a badass. Eating sardines from the can is just that. Look at yourself in the mirror. See the badass waiting to burst out. Look at an open can of sardines. What would a badass do? Whimper and scrunch up his/her nose? No, he or she would gulp it down and yell for more. You will habituate over time. It's how the brain works. You're in charge.

Second, you need to appreciate everything sardines offer you: mega convenience, super nutrition, and cheap food that saves you so much money you'll be able to retire early.

Third, give yourself time. We all need time to get used to flavors we're not used to, though I will tell you straight up that sardines are not that offensive. The smoked ones even remind me of tuna. (Tip: the smaller the sardine, the milder the flavor.) So, if you open up a can of sardines and there are three fat ones in it, you might brace yourself. However, if you open the can and you see 4 to 5 thinner sardines, then dive in with gusto. Remember, sometimes it just takes time to like something. It might take 10 or 20 servings of sardines for you to get more accustomed to them. It'll happen though, I promise.

Last, you need recipes that help you transition. The recipes aren't always completely carnivore, but they're still on the "dirty" carnivore side of things. In other words, you'll be mixing in just a few strong-flavored extras, in small amounts, to get you used to sardines. Things like mustard, hot sauce, relish, balsamic vinegar, capers, olives, etc. Over time, you can ease off these completely if desired. I now eat sardines straight most of the time, but heck, sometimes I add a dab of hot sauce or I add pickle relish or a squirt of mustard. I'm still considered a carnivore!

## Recipes

Let's dive into some sardine-based recipes that are frugal and mostly carnivore. These recipes assume that you have at least some fondness for sardines. If you don't, occasionally review the last section to get motivated. If you're one of the lucky folks who already loves sardines, well then high-five!

I generally eat sardines in one of four ways:

- Plain from the can
- With hot sauce
- With pickle relish
- With mustard

However, my family likes when I do the following with them. You can try the following recipes as is, or add some condiments.

## Sardine in a Salami "Taco" Shell

I grew up loving salami. When I was little, I would put a piece of salami in my mouth and suck all the fat and juice out of it, and then leave it packed down in the side of my mouth for hours, like chewing tobacco. On occasion, I'd fall asleep like this, and mom would come into my room at night and use her index finger to swipe (check) my mouth for a dried-out ball of salami. Thanks, mom!

- 1 can sardines, drained
- 3 to 4 slices salami

1. Place each sardine into a piece of salami and hold the salami closed at the top. Eat it like a mini-taco.

**Ham-Rolled Sardine "Burritos"**

My daughter is a fan of this combo. She'll eat sardines straight and plain but she doesn't love them. I'd say she *tolerates* them very well. However, when she eats them like this, she actually requests more.

- 1 can sardines, drained
- 3 to 4 slices ham

1. Roll each sardine in a piece of ham so it's like a burrito.

## Sardines on Eggs with Hot Sauce

I routinely make this for my husband's breakfast. He's a genuine sardine fan and will even drink the juices from the can. He's a badass, what can I say? Here, though, see how he likes them on eggs.

- 3 to 4 eggs, fried or scrambled
- 1 can sardines, drained
- Hot sauce

1. Plate the eggs and top them with sardines and hot sauce.

Variation: Make 3 eggs, add a slice of cheese while cooking them. Then plate them and top with sardines and hot sauce. My husband is particularly excited when I include gooey melted cheese.

### Melted Cheesy Sardines

This is a frugal carnivore variation of a recipe from one of my other books, *Recipes with Sardines.*

- 2 cans sardines, drained
- 1/4 cup shredded mozzarella or cheddar cheese

1. Put the sardines in an oven-safe dish. A ramekin is perfect.
2. Add the cheese.
3. Place the oven-safe dish under the broiler (or in a toaster oven) for a few minutes to warm the sardines and melt the cheese.

### Surf-n-Turf

It's a popular combo - fish and beef. But this time, it's cheap!

- 1 can sardines, drained and chopped
- 1/2 pound (8 ounces) ground beef
- salt, to taste

1. Season the ground beef with salt.
2. Add the ground beef to a small skillet and cook the ground beef, crumbling it with a spatula as it cooks.
3. Once the beef is almost cooked to your liking, add the sardines and cook until the beef has reached your desired temperature and the sardines are warmed through.

Chapter 6

# CONCLUSION

As you can see, eating a frugal carnivore diet is possible and I love it. It took me a month of experimenting with various ways to cook beef and figure out how to incorporate eggs and sardines for a well-rounded and fun experience. Use these tips to guide you to your own frugal carnivore experience. Even if you can't always find these ingredients and foods for the cheap prices I've found, the carnivore diet is no doubt much more frugal if you follow the general guidelines in this book.

I'd love to hear your frugal carnivore stories and experiences! Please email me at Kristen@HappySexyMillionaire.me to share.

## FREE PDF

**For a free, printable .PDF of the recipes in this book, email me at:**

**kristen@HappySexyMillionaire.me**

### Did you enjoy this book? If so, please leave a review!

As an independent author, your reviews are extremely helpful in getting the word out. After you leave a review, please drop me a line at kristen@HappySexyMillionaire.me so I can thank you!

### Other books by Kristen Suzanne

**Coffee Self-Talk:** *5 Minutes a Day to Start Living Your Magical Life* (under the name Kristen Helmstetter)

**The Carnivore Diet Handbook**

**Carnivore Diet Intermittent Fasting**

**Sardine Solution**

**Recipes with Sardines**

**Bone Broth Benefits & Easy Bone Broth Recipes**

## K. SUZANNE'S ROMANCE NOVELS

*Under the pen name, Brisa Starr*

**Lockdown Love**

**His Secret**

**Save Me**

**Sweet as Pie**

**Fake It** (September 2020)

Kristen's blog at: HappySexyMillionaire.me

Twitter: @KristensRaw

Instagram: Kristen_Helmstetter

Manufactured by Amazon.ca
Bolton, ON

34108547R00028